You're Worth The Wait

A Young Ladies Guide to Godly Dating

By

Kimberly G. Bosket

All scripture quotations was taking from Life in the Spirit Study Bible Zondervan Copyright 1992, 2003

Definitions came from American Heritage Webster Dictionary

Published by:

Divine Purpose Publishing

Printed in the United States of America

Printed on Recycled Paper

Published April 2011

Contents

Preface

The purpose of "You're Worth the Wait" is to help the young ladies of today's society discover their true value and worth and realize that they are jewels that are priceless. Proverbs 31:10 ask, "Who can find a virtuous woman? For her worth is far above rubies." I, Kimberly Bosket have been commissioned by God to live a life of purification and holiness to God. "I beseech ye brethren by the mercies of God that you present your bodies as a living sacrifice holy and acceptable to God, which is your reasonable service" (Romans 12:1). My life has been set apart to not only give God's Word, but to live God's Word. In a world full of so much perversion, God is calling our youth to answer the divine call that is upon their life, to live a life that is separated from sin, and not to compromise their standard in Christ. By the grace of God he has commissioned me to take that stand, and to stand in the gap for the youth; to proclaim that this is not the unknown generation, but the NOW (No Other Way) generation, because the Bible says that "Jesus is the way, the truth and the life and no man can come to the Father except by him" (John 14:6). The Bible also says in the book of 2nd Peter "We are a chosen generation, a royal priesthood, a holy nation that you may proclaim the praises of Him who called you out of darkness into the marvelous light." The Bible instructs us "not to be conformed to this world but to be ye transformed by the renewing of our mind." *God will raise up a nation that will obey Him, and God has commanded me to be an example for our young ladies and to help them find their true identity. I am persuaded that my mission in life is not to be popular with this world but to be holy and separated for the Master's use. We declare war on the devil and we decree that enough is enough; young lady you are worth the wait.*

Foreword

I met Kim several years ago when I was transferred to a different facility in my work place. It was an unwanted move with many lies and unpleasant emotions attached to it. When I arrived there the devil had already sat up shop and was ready for business. God had shown me the move and the place had a reputation for being ungodly. I met much unfair opposition, but there was this light forever shining and the light was Kim. There were people there who professed Christianity that were much older than Kim, but I saw no light. In fact these were the main ones aiding the enemy in my purposed demise. When the enemy saw the light in Kim that continued to give me strength to carry on, he turned on her. She was such a righteous young Christian that I wanted to know more about her. She shared some of her life story with me such as being raised in a Godly home with her grandparents etc. As I watched Kim stand tall in the face of adversity and never waver in her walk with Christ, I gained more strength in my walk and more respect for her as a Christian. She was transferred after awhile, but we kept in touch. Once you come in contact with a light so bright you want to stay in it. I continued to stand against the enemy and soon the Lord turned it around for me. Some of the people that came up against me became friends and some have even joined together with me in Bible study groups. I thank God for Kim. I know I would have not overcome if she had not been there, but her love for God and me made it so much easier. She is a chosen vessel of God, and when she told me she was writing a book to encourage young women to live Godly through

Christ, I knew this would be another outpouring of God's anointing on his lost or hurting sheep.

"My people are destroyed because of a lack of knowledge" (Hosea 4:6). It takes a village is a popular African proverb. It embraces the premise that every member in the village has a personal responsibility to see that each child gets what he or she needs to become a well-rounded individual. This concept should extend to every community that children inhabit, regardless of race, creed, ethnicity or socioeconomic status.

This is a superb account of a Spirit filled Christian woman that has responded to her call and responsibility as a member of the village. She exposes the elusive tactics of the enemy; the enemy who ultimately sets traps that destroy the very fabric of the village, causing it to rip into many pieces and allowing the precious contents to fall into a dangerous abyss from which some never recover. Some of the traps include unwanted pregnancies, abortions, neglected and abused children, and sexually transmitted diseases, including HIV/ AIDS. The tree to life experience and biblical solutions act as needful thread and patch work needed to sew together the rips that must be repaired in order to save our village and the souls of its people. Knowledge is power and this is a knowledge-filled and easy to read book, both for learning and living. God Bless you as you read and study. May you find your avenue of responsibility in the village?

Mother Dorothy Anderson
Pentecostal Temple Revival

Dedication

This book is dedicated to the life of my two angels, Joe and Geneva Smith (now deceased) who did not allow their age or their physical body to stop them but accepted the divine call that was on their life to raise me, and counted it not robbery to give me not 100 percent, but 110 percent. They gracefully took on the task of raising me in the fear and admonition of the Lord. They taught me how to respect not only my elders, but to respect myself. Thank you for allowing God to use you to make an impartation that has changed my destiny.

I love you Grandma and Granddaddy.

Prologue

My name is Kimberly Bosket. I am thirty-two years old, the wife of Elder Brian Bosket and the mother of two. I have been saved since I was thirteen years old. I was raised by my two grandparents (now deceased) who were sent from God to introduce me to a man; my best friend, my comforter, my deliverer; Jesus the Christ, the greatest gift of all. My grandparents Joe and Geneva Smith raised me in a Godly home. When I came to them, my grandfather was sixty-seven-years old and my grandmother was in her late forties or early fifties. My grandparents were wonderful. My grandmother believed in me and loved me with an unconditional love, and all I wanted to do was make them happy. When I walked out that door, it wasn't about me; I represented my grandparents and everything they stood for. I did not want to shame them. I remember people in the neighborhood saying, "Mrs. Smith, Kim is so respectful." Well, I had better been if I wanted to live. Grandma was a strong lady and you just didn't play any games. Granddaddy was also tough too. He was a tall 250-pound man who lived a full life. Even in his latter years he would still be outside mowing the yard, feeding the dog, and hauling trash to the dumpster. He used to take me to the houses where he used to mow yards. I would just be on the back of the truck singing.

I grew up in a small town called Wauchula. A town where every body knew everybody's name, I used to go to the grocery store with no shoes on. Can you imagine? If I did that in the city somebody would call the Department of Children and Families. But for me that was the norm; that's probably the reason my feet grew so big. God really blessed me. I had a very good life there and I was known as the "little girl that be preaching and singing. Preacher Kim."

My life has never been the same since that day, November 3, 1991, when I accepted Jesus Christ as my personal savior. I remember that day all so well. Pastor Victor was preaching and I started crying, but I didn't think I was crying because of God. I just started weeping and Pastor Victor said when I got up there to the altar, "I know that you are for real because you are crying." But I really didn't understand what was happening and at that time I really didn't want to get saved that Sunday. But I decided to go up there anyway because everybody else did it. At that time they had these born again certificates. It was a little piece of paper that had the date you got saved as a reminder, and although I didn't realize what was happening, that one step of faith opened a door that has changed my life forever. I used to take my Bible to school everyday. I would walk down the halls singing loud. I was not ashamed of this gospel at all, and everyday after class I would tell my whole class I loved them. I know they must have thought that I was crazy, but I didn't care, I was in Love with Jesus. I have had many mentors in my life and one of my greatest mentors was my uncle Hosea. Uncle Hosea was like my father, he did everything that my seventy-year-old granddaddy couldn't do. He made sure I stayed out of trouble. He taught me how to play basketball, and took me to the tennis court. And he took the time out to talk to me about the boys and to beware of different traps they may try to set for me. He used tell me different stories about guys and create different scenarios for me to think about it. Actually he raised my self- awareness about what kind of guy I wanted, and what kind of guy I did not want. He was very knowledgeable in the Word of God too. He also was the jokester of the family, always playing jokes and making faces. I remember one Christmas I was about 13 he gave me and my cousin Sharhonda a gift. So we thought we had a good gift, only to unwrap it and discover that it was a Bible. You should have seen our faces; boy were we disappointed. We said, "A Bible. We don't want a Bible." He said, "But that's what you need." Uncle Hosea was such a clown, he also had other gifts, a basketball for me and a radio for my cousin, but the Bible has taken me so much farther than the basketball has. He also used to wrap up old pots and pans as a prank and give them as gifts.

Before I gave my life to the Lord I was rebellious, hateful, and I was headed down a dark road full of destruction and I didn't understand my purpose. I was very angry and bitter. I remember this prophet had come and he prophesied to me. He said, "You have been very bad, but you're going to do better aren't you"? And I said, "yes sir." I know God is a good God because he came and rescued me from myself. I was messed up, that's the reason why it is so important that our young people give their lives to the Lord early because just like God has a plan for your life, the devil does too. So, we don't have time to say we are too young, because more and more young people are dying everyday. I often times say that God had to save me at early age to spare my life. I was one of those hard cases, and if it weren't for me accepting Jesus the Christ as my personal savior as early as I did I would have been either dead or in prison by now. I can't promise you that you won't go through trials because they come with the territory, but I can promise you that God will keep you through every trial if you trust in Him. For the Bible says that many are the afflictions of the righteous but the Lord delivereth him out of them all. (Psalm 34:19) I have had a lot of challenges in this life, yet I do not regret one day that I have been saved. My motto is simply "One day at a time". Every day has not always been up for me but I can truly say that every day with Jesus gets sweeter than the day before. Let me now say "If it had not been for the Lord on my side; (Psalm 94:17) Lord have mercy, I thank God I am saved." I am not saying that because it sounds good but that is just the God's heaven truth. Every since the tender age of thirteen I knew God called me to work with youth. I used to take the neighborhood kids and sing with them in the street and teach them the Bible. I would throw little parties with them. Basically I took the time to invest in them. Our young people need to know that they are special and that they are worth you taking time out with them. Although I was much older than them, I didn't mind because I enjoyed just teaching and spending time with them. Everyday groups of them would come over and knock on the door, and ask, "Mr. Joe, Kim home?" and ninety-nine percent of the time I was right there back in my room. I truly represented the term "home girl", because my grandparents didn't play about you ripping and running all over the place. The farthest I ever went was to the stop sign and that was at the end of the road. I was always within calling distance.

Somebody once said that the way you find your passion in life is to ask yourself a question; what is it that you would do all the time at any time even if you didn't get paid for it? Some of you may say I like to sing, write, enjoy working on computers or working with kids. Whatever it is, that's how you discover your passion. Another way to discover your purpose and passion is to find out what bothers you. What makes you upset to the point if you had the power you would change it? God has given each of us a purpose and gift to be used to glorify His name.

Acknowledgements

I would like to first give honor to God who is the author and finisher of my faith. He is so faithful. I thank Him for His promises and His word, for truly He is my everything; the air I breathe, the song I sing. He is my all. I would like to thank God for my husband, the father of my children, my friend and lover, Elder Brian Bosket. Thank you for believing in me and always being my biggest cheerleader. Thank you for loving God more than you love me and being a Godly example for our children and me. You are full of wisdom and great power and I thank God that I am able to share my life with you. You are the epitome of what a man is and I love you. I would also like to thank God for my Bishop and First lady Dr. Darnell and Elaine Mack of Agape Worship Center, Fort Lauderdale, Florida. There is no other church in the world that can compare to Agape. Thank you Bishop for preaching the unadulterated word of God. Thank you for taking a stand against sin, no matter whose feet you step on. From the White House to the Poor house, you never compromised God's word. Thank you for teaching men how to love their wives and be faithful. First Lady, I believe that when Proverbs 31 was written, they must have had you in mind. You are the exact representative of the virtuous woman. Your smile and generous spirit can change any atmosphere. You have been an example to me from the first time I met you. I love you. I want to thank my mother, Geneather Ashby. She's my twin although she doesn't think so. Mom, thank you for just being you. Thank you for teaching me about life and helping me to open my eyes about people and certain things. I know you got my back. I love you and I appreciate you.

I also would like to acknowledge Mother Dorothy Anderson, thank you for believing in me and being a spiritual guide to me after my grandmother passed away. I would like to thank Ms. Cora Mae Hudson for taking out the time to take me to church and being a great role model for young ladies to follow. I would like to thank God for Pastor Deloris Williams for being a great mentor and Godmother. To my mentor Uncle Hosea, thank you for being that father figure for me. Thank you for taking time out with me to teach me how to play basketball and tennis. Thank you for those long conversations about life. I love you. To Aunt Candie, my friend, my mentor, I thank you for all those inspirational talks about the Lord. I thank you for praying for me, and just being an example to all of us. Truly God has smiled on you and the best is yet to come. To my cousin Gwinnett, my big cousin, girl you know you mean so much to me. I look up to you. I am encouraged by your faith and your strength. I am so glad you are not only my blood cousin, but also my sister in Christ. Thank you, I love you girl. There are so many people that have made impartations in my life and I pray that I have not left anyone out, but if I have, I want to say thank you to everyone that has ever prayed for me or made an impartation in my life. I love you all.

Chapter One

Lies Exposed /Truth Revealed

It's time for you to know the truth about sex. God created sex and He ordained it. In the book of Genesis, Chapter 3, the Bible says that God told Adam that He would make him a helpmeet. Someone he could relate to. So He gave him Eve. He put Adam in a deep sleep and took Eve out of him. Then He put them in the garden, and He told them to have dominion, and He told them to be fruitful and multiply. Now, at that time they were innocent. They did not know what sin was. God told them that you shall eat of every tree except the tree of knowledge of good and evil. See, God never intended for us to know anything else but good. The Bible says that Satan was also in the garden and began to talk with Eve. Of course, Eve didn't know that the enemy was deceiving her. So when the devil began to talk to her, she fell into his trap like so many of us. We don't realize what we don't know can hurt us. We need to be equipped with the knowledge of the word of God so that when anything comes against us that do not line-up with what the Word says, we can combat it. A lot of young ladies didn't know how having premarital sex affects you, and had they known the effects of it, they probably would have considered waiting. Don't let the devil deceive you into thinking that God is against you having sex and that God is just trying to keep you from having fun. That's a lie! God wants what's best for you, and He knows what's best for you. Before Adam and Eve ate the fruit they didn't even know they were naked. But when they ate of it, they received knowledge.

When God came through the garden, he asked Adam where was he, and he stated, "I was hiding from you because I was naked." Young ladies, nobody is supposed to see you naked but your husband unfortunately some young ladies did not give it up, some young ladies were molested and raped but you have to understand that it was not your fault you were not supposed to be exposed. That's why so many young ladies feel violated because someone other than their husband have seen a part of them that was supposed to be kept private. God asked Adam, "Who told you that you were naked?" God didn't want anyone influencing your decisions but Him because He knew that once sin entered the world it would be much suffering and pain. God gives us a free will, and He sets before you life and death, but He gives you the answer; He says choose life. (Deuteronomy 30:19)

Chapter Two

YOU'RE WORTHY

Solomon asked a question in Proverbs 31:10, "Who can find a virtuous woman? For her worth is far more than rubies." This let's me know that I have to first be found, and then when I am found, the man must know my value in order to appreciate me. Before he finds me however, I must know my value first because no one is going to appreciate and value you if you don't know your value. Somebody is looking for you, they want you, but the question is, what do they want you for? That's what you have to ask yourself. Young ladies *you are worthy*. You are worth waiting for. You are worth the respect and honor of a man. Let's identify the word worth. Worth means to have value, to esteem high. If you don't know the value of a thing you will abuse it. So many young ladies do not know their worth. They base their worth on how a man treats them, or maybe how a man may have treated their mother or someone close to them. You need to know that you are worth more than a #4 special on a fast food restaurant menu. You are worth more than a full set of nails, eyelashes, a paid cell phone bill, hairdos and/or jewelry. Did you know that jewelry is not real anyway? The real gold is going to be in heaven where the streets are paved with gold. Too many young ladies are settling for these things in order to feel worthy. Yet, this does not make you feel worthy, it often times leaves a void. Because after he has paid your cell phone bill or had your nails done, you are still trying to figure out why he's unfaithful. So all of the stuff he buys for you doesn't mean anything. If your heart is broken, if you don't have his respect, you don't have anything. A worthy young lady needs a worthy young man, somebody who is worth you even talking to. Some guys are not even worth you entertaining. Don't waste your time on dead weight. You need someone who knows their self-worth and not only will love you, but will love God more than you. The Bible says love God with all your heart, mind and soul, and then you can love your neighbors and others. (Deuteronomy 6:5) Be leery of the guy that says, "I love you more than anything and if I lost you I wouldn't survive." These types of relationships are not healthy; nevertheless, many girls are falling into this trap. The guy makes you think he is so in love with you, but it is a matter of control and possession. In some cases, young ladies have lost their lives due to the possessiveness when they have decided to exit the relationship. There is absolutely no way a man can truly love you without knowing God first, because God is Love, and you can't have love without God. He is the author and finisher of the word love and everything about love originates from Him.

We are living in a day and time where young women will have sex with anybody at any cost. Since many young ladies want to be accepted, they will sacrifice one of the greatest gifts that God has given them; their body. The Bible says that your body is the temple of the Holy Ghost (1Corinthian 6:19) it is where God dwells and moves; he wants to live inside of you and use you for his Glory. The word virgin used to be considered honorable; now in today's society it is considered a curse word. When I was in school, if a girl was having sex in high school, she was not cool. In other words, being a virgin was in, and if you were not, you were not accepted. Unfortunately today, if you haven't done it by the time you are in middle school then, you are alienated and criticized. Something is wrong. Our elementary school kids are experiencing some things that are just unbelievable. They are so in tuned to the latest songs on the radio, the latest videos on television, but it is hard for them to remember a paragraph in their school textbook. Our society calls wrong right, and right wrong. It is a crying shame how perverted our world has gotten. The devil is nothing but a copycat and a creator of nothing. He takes the good things that God has created and perverts it. Everything that God has created is good, Satan has tried to use it as a tool of destruction; such as sex. Sex is a good thing. It was ordained by God, but when sex is not used between a husband and a wife, it contaminates the purpose it was originally designed for. The Internet, which is a very useful tool, has brought millions of families back together. It makes going to school easier and so much more; nevertheless, in the hands of the wrong person it can be used as a detrimental device. The television was also created good, but look at everything that is on TV these days. I find it very uncomfortable to watch a PG movie with my six- year -old daughter. And let's take a look at the rainbow. The rainbow is a sign, a promise that God made with Noah that he would not destroy the earth with water, but fire next time. So every time you look at the rainbow it represents a promise that God made. Regardless, how many people think about God's promise when they see a person driving a car with a sticker that has the colors of a rainbow? Immediately we say that person is a homosexual or that person is a lesbian, but the rainbow was not created for that purpose. You can rest assure that the devil is a liar, and it's God's word that will stand. For the Bible declares let every man be a liar, but God's word is true. (Romans 3:4) The devil will throw all types of deceptions but stay focused and believe only what the word of God says. I remember when I was about eleven years old, Granddaddy who was about seventy at the time said, "Well Kim, you know them boys will get you pregnant and say the baby isn't theirs." I said, "No boy is going to get me pregnant and say the baby isn't his." Granddaddy would just leave it like that. He wanted to give me something to think about. Those nuggets he used to throw at me opened my eyes, and made me become more aware of my worth. The Bible says in Jeremiah 29:11, "I know the thoughts I have toward you thoughts that are good and not evil to give you an expected end." What kind of future do you plan for yourself? Is your future filled with dreams of success, or are you just living and saying whatever happens is going to happen? If you are thinking this way, change your mindset and think success. No matter what your past looks like, God wants you to excel in life. God wants to give you a man that will not only meet your material needs, but also your spiritual needs. He wants to give you someone that can pick you up in spirit. There are times when I am down and just feeling a little depressed, and my husband will just ask are you okay. And even though I may say I'm fine he knows that something is wrong, and although he may not say anything, after a little while my spirit has changed, and I know that he was praying for me. God wants to give you someone who will treat you like a queen, not so that you can worship the man, but so that you can worship the God that gave you the man. Don't make a permanent decision on a temporary situation. As a young person you will encounter all types of guys that will come your way. Some will be good, some will be bad, but always seek to know their motives, and why they were sent into your life. Are they there to build you up or tear you down? I learned at an early age to bless God when they come and bless God when they go. I see so many young ladies dealing with low self-esteem, bitterness and loneliness. A lot of us grew up without our natural parents, and depending on the situation, you still may be dealing with the hurt, but if you are searching trying to find your worth, don't look to the magazines, television, or music videos to discover your worth. I know that our society bombards us with what they call beauty, but you don't see the great price that a lot of those young ladies have to pay in order to be down. They are abused, mistreated and tossed around like a piece of bread. There's no telling how many guys they had to sleep with to get where they are. It is just not worth it, no matter how much fame you think you want; true success only comes from God. For the Bible also says that as you meditate on God's word day and night and observe to do all that is in the Bible, then will your way be made prosperous and then will you have good success (Joshua 1:8). The Bible also says that Satan is the god of this world, (Ephesians 2:2) meaning lowercase g, because there are many idol gods, but there is only one true and living God. Satan is the one who is in the atmosphere and the air trying to influence our young people and trying to take control of their minds so that they can yield to him, and serve him. But God said he would raise up a nation that will obey Him, in spite of what the enemy is trying to achieve. There are some young people that are committed to God and not willing to compromise. This society can be so cruel and difficult to live in, especially if you are trying to be a Christian. I remember being called names, and the guys would say, oh something must be wrong with you, but I didn't care because I knew that I was doing what was right even if it was not popular. You cannot allow what the world says to you to define you, only God can do that. For example, if you had a car and it needed to be repaired, would you take your car to the tile company to find out what's wrong with your car? I would hope not. What does a tile company know about cars? No, you'll take it back to the manufacturer or the one who knows about the car, and that's how it is with our young people. When you are trying to seek guidance; don't seek advice from people who are trying to learn just like you. Go to your manufacturer, your creator Jesus Christ. He is the only one who is qualified to tell you who you are. He is the manufacturer and you are the product. If God's "word doesn't confirm it, don't you accept it." My Bishop teaches us that you have what you approve of. You need a personal relationship with Him. Also, look to a positive role model, someone you can pattern your life after. Young ladies, you are so valuable to God, but you must become valuable to yourself. If you had a gold necklace that cost $1600.00, wouldn't you be careful of where you leave it? Or, if your deceased mom or dad left you something that was very dear to you; wouldn't you try to take care of it? That's just how you should view yourself. Please listen, make them wait, you're worth it. Let me tell you a little story that changed my life. I always wanted to be a challenge. I remember I was about eight or nine and this little boy asked me a question; "Do you like me? Check yes or no. Will you go out with me? Check yes or no." Well, I didn't check either. I asked him a question; "Why do you want to go out with me?" He could not answer that question and some years later he said to me, "I'll never ask you to go out with me again." Then he asked, "Why did you ask me when we were younger, why I wanted to go out with you?" I told him, "I wanted to know what it was about me that you liked and what made me different from other girls," but that was too deep for him. He couldn't answer the question and it kind of made him uncomfortable. But hey, I knew that there were girls prettier than me, so I wanted him to discover me, but he just wanted to be able to say I was his girlfriend. I didn't have time for that in all honesty. Anyway, most worthy guys like a challenge. They don't want anyone they can easily get. Make them work for you. Know your worth and let them discover who you are on the inside, not the outside or sexually.

Chapter Three

Know The Man Before the man

The Bible says "know no man after the flesh, but by the spirit" (2 Corinthians 5:16). The only way you can really determine a man is by his spirit. That's why you have to know God before the man. God will reveal unto you every counterfeit that comes your way. I remember countless times when the enemy tried to send imposters my way. He knew that the gangsters and dope dealers didn't have a chance, so he sent men in suits and ties to try to deceive me, but by the grace of God, their true colors were always revealed. I remember one time in particular, when I was about 18, I was at a church function and this man came up to me and introduced himself. He asked, "Your name Kim Smith?" I said yes. We began talking about the Lord, and how good He was. Mind you, this man was about 30 years old at the time. Anyway, I used to work at Eckerd, and he started coming in there very frequently. I didn't think anything of it because we were just talking about God. Little did I know the devil had put out an assignment on my life for him to deceive me. Well to make a long story short, I had been telling Brian (friend) about him so he told me to ask him why he keeps coming around. That was the best thing I could have ever done, because two days later he came to my job and I was standing outside. I waited for him to come out the door, and when he did he said, "You didn't see me when I walked in?" I said, "I saw you." He then asked, "Why you didn't say anything?" I immediately asked him, "How did you find out about me?" He said, "You don't remember when you were preaching in Arcadia, Florida?" I said, "Yes, but I don't remember you." He began to get very offensive and responded, by saying, "You have abused our friendship and all I have tried to be to you is a friend." Still angry, he then said, "I don't want to sleep with you Kimberly." Well the Bible says, "out of the abundance of the heart the mouth speaketh," (Matthew 12:34), so that was in his heart. My answer to him was, "I didn't say anything about you sleeping with me." In actuality that was his plan. He saw me as being young and vulnerable, and I was on his hit list. He was exposed, and his motives were revealed that day. After that he never talked to me nor came to my job again.

Young ladies, you have to stay connected to God. God will provide a way of escape. The Bible declares, "There is no temptation that is common unto man that God has not provided a way of escape."(1 Corinthians 10:13). You have to look out for the signs because the Bible says don't be ignorant of the devices of the devil. (2 Corinthians 2:11) He will try and destroy you if you are not aware. Get to know God before you get to know a man. If all you have ever known is natural man, after natural man you won't know what to do. When you don't have a man, if you have ever experienced Christ, you will never be the same. Christ is the model that is to be used to choose a mate. He must look like God, meaning his characteristics should be just like God. I know you may be thinking nobody is perfect, but God does not want you to settle for anything less than His best. It's just some things my husband can't do for me. Now amongst flesh, there's no other man on this planet that can compare to my husband, but when it comes to My God, it's no competition. There are many times I just need him to usher me into the presence of God. I knew God before I knew my husband therefore I know what it is like to spend time with God and be satisfied in his presence. God was there for me when my heart was broken. He was there for me when I didn't know what to do and I was unclear about my future. He has healed me of past wounds and hurts that I thought I could not endure, like when I lost my grandfather in 2001 and then lost my grandmother in 2002. Only God could soothe my pain. How did I get through that? My soul still looks back and wonders where did me and my cousin Letisha get the strength to plan our grandmother's funeral without losing our mind. It was nobody but God. The Bible says, "He will never leave you nor forsake you." (Hebrew 13:5) This is the key to your relationship and piece of mind. If you don't remember anything else in this book, don't ever forget this, fall in love with Jesus. Please, use God's word against everything that your potential mate is telling you. If God says don't fornicate and he wants to fornicate he's not the one because he's asking you to sin against God, and that could lead you into destruction. If he really loves you like he's telling you he loves you, he'll wait. If he can't wait, it's up to you; you must break it off. The reason why we have so many bad relationships is because when we fall in love the man becomes our everything and we put the man before the real and true man; JESUS. There is a certain place that God has designed for our husband and there is a certain place that God has set apart only for him, it is reserved. Keep everybody in his or her proper place in your life. The Bible says that "you were bought with a price you are not your own."(1Corinthians 6:20) Nobody died for you but Jesus. He purchased you with his own blood, and he is a jealous God, and anything you put before God will either disappoint you or be removed from your life. A lot of times we have to have our hearts broken, and our minds confused, before we realize that God must be first. Listen, my favorite song is "Can't Nobody Do Me Like Jesus." It is a true song. *I have searched all over and I can't find anybody. I went to the east I went to the west but I done find out that he is the very best. I went to the north I went to the south I gave it over to Jesus and he worked it out*. I love my husband. He is truly a man of God, but he doesn't have the ability to love me like Jesus, although, through Christ I know he does his best. What I'm really trying to say is if you keep God in the center, a man may come and go, but God will always heal you and preserve you in the midst of adversity.

Chapter Four

WHY WAIT?

Somebody may be asking the question, "Why should I wait to have sex until I get married?" I know that sometimes it is not enough to just say wait. Our society does not promote abstinence and definitely doesn't support marriage. The first reason to wait is that the Bible says "Flee from youthful lust, and avoid fornication. (2 Timothy 2:22)" Listen, nobody is worth you dying and losing your soul for. You may just look at having sex before marriage as being casual. There are a lot of consequences involved in it, spiritually, emotionally, and physically. Spiritually, your relationship with God is affected. God loves us and He desires to be in fellowship with us, but when we sin, the fellowship is hindered. It's not until we repent that we can commune with God.

Second, emotionally so many relationships are destroyed through sex. Does this sound typical to you? Young girls get pregnant by guys and when you ask them are they with the father, most of the time the answer is "No, we broke up." That is emotionally disruptive to a person because you are still tied to that person through sexual intercourse, and the more partners you have, the more mental challenges you may have to face. The Bible says when you have sex with someone you become one with that person. (1 Corinth 6:16) Whatever is in you enters them, so if they are dealing with low self-esteem, depression or even suicidal thoughts, you may find yourself experiencing the same types of behaviors. God is the only one that can clean you and make you whole again, free of all those spirits. The third reason is physical consequences. Diseases such as Chlamydia, PID, Herpes, and Gonorrhea can cause physical problems that may be detrimental. Please educate yourself on these types of diseases if you are considering having sex. Sin has a cost attached to it. Are you willing to pay the price? I know as young people we don't think long term. We only live for the moment. For example, a 16-year-old boy gets a 15-year-old girl pregnant. Now at the time they really didn't want the responsibility of being parents; they just wanted to have a good time. Here it is ten years later, that relationship is long over, but now he meets a young lady who he wants to marry and then spend the rest of his life with. But guess what, he has to tell his future wife that he has a child and now that child has to become a part of their family. If they marry, this may include the wife having to help take care of that child if the father has to pay child support. Sometimes it's multiple children involved from prior relationships. Don't misunderstand me, children are a blessing from the Lord, but God has a perfect plan for your life. The devil has a plan also. Whose plan for your life will you follow?

The enemy doesn't show you your future; he only shows you what it is for a moment. This happens everyday. Don't think short term, think long term. Wouldn't you like to be your husband's only baby momma? I know that this seems obsolete, but nothing is impossible with God. We all have lust in us and if we do not have any self-control, our very lust and appetites will destroy us. God has created a place and time for us to satisfy our lust, and that is with our husband. You want to be able to have sex without the feeling of guilt and shame, and in marriage you will have that. You can do it as many times as you would like. Another reason why you should consider waiting is because of the AIDS epidemic. This disease is horrific. It is taking out so many of our youth, which is so disturbing. This disease will take a mother away from her daughter, a son away from his father. Imagine growing up without your father or mother because of a choice that they made in life. Do you think they meant to hurt you, and leave you without ever confirming your identity? No, at that time they didn't even know the consequences of their action. Well, I had to deal with this question a lot of nights, because when I was 15 I lost my father. I had to grow up not knowing him, and it was hard because I needed to identify with him so that I could feel secure. He has two beautiful grandchildren that he never got to hold, nor hear them say "Granddaddy."

I often hear my Bishop say your childhood can affect your adulthood, and that is so true. What happened to you, as a child may be the very reason why you behave the way you do, but your past does not have to destroy your future. He also says that it takes a man to affirm a boy's identity and it takes a woman to affirm a girl's identity. In spite of an old popular saying, your mother cannot be both the mother and the father of that home. A mother has her role, and the father has his role too. What does a father know about that time of the month? He can't relate. What does a mother know about what boys have to go through in their bodies? I know that most of our single mothers have been trying to handle that, but the truth is, a mother can only do what a mother was designed to do. If that father is not there, you have to trust in the Lord and ask God to put someone in his or her life to help him or her fill that void. The Bible says that love is patient, which lets me know that we don't have to hurry genuine love. 1 (Corinthians 13:4) It is patient; lust on the other hand is right now, give it to me now. There is something wrong with that, anything worth having requires some waiting. We live in a society that says if you love me, you will have sex with me to make me happy, but that's contrary to the Word of God. Love is longsuffering. When you're waiting on your worthy man, you have to suffer. You may have to give up some of your girlfriends who may not be trying to do what you're doing. If you are going to wait you cannot be watching X-rated movies on TV or going out by yourself late at night. Go out into groups and don't allow him to touch you inappropriately. You also may find yourself alone because everybody may not understand the stand that you are taking to wait. No suffering at the present time is joyous, but in the end it produces much fruit. Waiting can be a good way to wean out the good guys from the bad guys. Let me share a quick story. I remember this guy who my friend had given my phone number. About three or four days later, to my surprise he called me. We began to just talk. I introduced myself to him, and he introduced himself to me. His name was Clifford. In the middle of us talking about different things, I said to him, "You know I'm saved." He said, "You saved?" I said, "Yes." He said, "You don't look like you are saved." I got offended and asked, "What do you mean, I don't look like I am saved?" We talked about ten or fifteen more minutes. Clifford lived about 15 to 20 miles away from me. I really thought the conversation was going good. He then asked me, "Hey, you ever caught a long distance pass?" I replied, "Yes, you know I used to play flag football in school." He said, "Well catch this," and he hung up the phone. I couldn't believe it. I sat there for a moment thinking maybe the phone hung-up by mistake, but he never called back. I realized that if we had been on the phone talking about when we could meet up or when he could "hit that", we would have been on the phone all night. I recognized he didn't want to get to know me for me; he wanted me added to his hit list. So I said thank you Lord for revealing to me his motives. See most guys don't want to wait because they feel like this is just a game, and the goal is to get as many girls as they can. I guess it does something for their ego, but guys are losing their life sooner than anticipated because of this sex game. I often hear my husband talk about when he was growing up and how important it was to be able to hang with the other guys. In order to be cool you had to do certain things like drink and have a lot of girlfriends. So he did it thinking that it was cool. They told the guys certain things like "the reason why you have so many bumps in your face is because you're not active sexually." Most often the guys started having sex only to find out that the bumps were still there. You see how our world is confused about what is right and wrong? There are many benefits of waiting; with the increase in sexually transmitted diseases and unwanted teenage pregnancies, it would be in your best interest to consider waiting.

Chapter Five

It's Not Too Late to Wait

The Bible says, "All have sinned and come short of the Glory of God" (1Corinthians 5:17). Well, you may be asking, "What if I have already had sex?" I say unto you, it's not too late to wait, and although you are not a virgin anymore, God still wants you to follow His plan that He designed for you in the beginning. The devil's job is to condemn you and make you feel like it's all over because of your past, but I want to encourage you. Young lady, get up and try it again, for the Bible says, "If any man be in Christ he is a new creature. Old things are passed away and all things become new." (2 Corinthian 5:17) The Bible also says that a righteous man falls seven times, but he gets back up. (Proverbs24: 16). Don't beat yourself up, however don't allow the enemy to make you feel like oh I can keep sinning and it's okay because God will forgive me. The Bible says, "Shall we continue in sin so that grace can abound God forbid."(Romans 6: 1) Although God forgives, there are still consequences for our actions. Still, God never condemns you. He only convicts you to compel you to come back into fellowship with Him, because sin separates you from God. Many young people find themselves back in fornication over and over again. The Bible says when a spirit departs from a man it comes back again and if it finds that the place it left is clean and hasn't been filled with anything else, then it brings back seven more demons and the last state of the man is worse than the beginning. (Matthew 12:43) That means that when you repent, to turn or have a change of mind, you must receive the Holy Ghost, which gives, you power (Acts 1:8).

It is the power of the Holy Spirit that helps us to resist sin. It is the key to your success as a Christian. Paul began to write in the book of (Romans7: 15) "That what I want to do that I do not and that that I don't want to do that's what I do." Paul said in the book of Romans "I saw another law working in my members."(Romans 7:23) Young ladies we are in spiritual warfare. You may wonder what I mean by that. It means there's no time to be unclear about your destiny in life. You are so important that the enemy is willing to do whatever it takes to destroy and kill you. That's the reason you have to equip yourself with the necessary tool to defeat him. You don't have to be a victim of your past. We have all made mistakes but God is concerned about your future. He wants you to enjoy your life in Him and live your life more abundantly. (John 10: 10) states, "I came that you may have life and have it more abundantly, but the thief cometh to steal, kill and to destroy." Everything God says you can have or ever be. Don't let him steal your future because of your past.

I hear a lot of people talk about how hard it is to wait. They say things like my flesh is burning and I need a man, but at what expense will you go to get one? My aunt Candie, another one of my mentors (one of the greatest if I must say) has been divorced for over thirteen years. She is a very attractive lady, so it isn't that she can't get a man. No, she doesn't want just any man. She wants the right man that God has for her. She told me not too long ago that she'd rather be by herself than to settle for someone just to have sex. It's more to life than sex young ladies. I asked her one time, "How do you do it?" She replied, "I keep my mind on Jesus. I don't watch certain things on TV and I don't go certain places that will put me in a compromising position. God will keep you if you want to be kept."

Chapter Six

LET HIM FIND YOU

The Bible says "He that finds a wife finds a good thing." (Proverbs 18:22) Let your mate find you, not just in location but also in the spirit. Allow him to get to know you. In order for that to take place you must get to know yourself. I'll tell anybody, I enjoyed my single life, because it is different when you get married. I mean you have to consider your husband. You may not be able to go as much as you used to when you were single. In other words, your responsibilities will change. You have to take care of the children and so many other things that come with being a wife.

Let me tell you the story that changed my life forever. In 1995 I was in the tenth grade and my teacher showed us a video of a man by the name of Dave Roever. He is currently a motivational speaker that goes into schools across the nation. He talked about how when he was in the war and a grenade blew his face off. His whole body was burned and things fell off, like his ear, fingers and other parts of his body. What changed me was when he said he was in the hospital and his wife came in there looking at what was left of her husband. She looked upon him and said, "Dave, I still love you." However, another man's wife looked at her husband lying there looking like a skeleton. She took off her ring, put it between his toes, and said, "I can't live like this," and walked away. Dave Roever said, "You know why my wife could look at me and say that? Because our relationship was not based on the back seat of a car but on our honesty, love and God."

Young ladies that's what you want. Ask yourself a question; "Do I and this person have a solid foundation so that if I lose my shape after having a couple of babies, or I get into a real bad accident this person will stay with me, or will he be like Dave's friend's wife and say, "I can't take this any more"? In order for you to have a relationship that's lasting, your foundation has to be solid as a rock and the only solid Rock I know is Jesus Christ. That's what I wanted; someone who wanted me for me, not my body, and the only way for me to know was for me not to have sex with him until marriage. Some will stay and some will go, but eventually if you don't give in most will go. Yet the Bible says "the race is not given to the swift nor the strong but he that endured until the end."(Ecclesiastes 9:11) You're Worth the Wait.

Young ladies you are a good thing, and when you know your self-worth, you won't settle for just anything or anybody. You know how it is when you are going for an interview, there are simply certain things that an employee looks for and if you don't meet their qualifications then you don't get the job. Some jobs require that you be 18 or older, have a high school diploma and that's it. Those qualifications may get you a job at McDonald's or a convenience store, but some job qualifications are greater. You may have to have a bachelor's degree or several years of experience or even a certain type of license, depending on the employer. Well, that is the same attitude you must have when dating. He must be qualified. He must love God with all his heart, mind, and soul. Otherwise, he doesn't even have the ability of loving you or even knowing how to treat you if he doesn't know Jesus and the love He has for you. He must be saved, sanctified, and filled with the Holy Ghost. I wouldn't even trust a man with me if he weren't saved. Furthermore, he must have a job, or be in the process of getting one. He must have a vision, for not only his life, but also your life together, for without a vision the people perish.

(Proverbs 29:18) This is the kind of man you want. The Bible says, "Charm is deceitful and beauty is passing but the woman who feared the Lord she shall be praised. Her husband praise and her children rise and call her blessed." (Proverbs 31:30) Any praise that is outside of the fear of God is not real praise and it is only temporary.

Chapter Seven

Holy Spirit: Can't Wait Without It

The nature of man is sinful. It's only when we allow the Holy Spirit to live in us that we can truly have a successful marriage. I hear people say, "Me and my husband have been together for 20 years and we never have been in an argument." I say to myself wow; they must be angels, and not humans, because I don't see how two people in the natural could never have any confrontation with each other. When a man or women is in the spirit, it's like a little heaven on earth; he or she is so awesome. My husband and me have had our good days and God knows we have had our bad. Please don't be deceived, unless the Lord builds the house you labor in vain. (Psalm 127:2) We have been laboring for nine years now and there are still so many things that God is still trying to perfect in us. Nevertheless, I can honestly say we have come a long way and I am expecting God to continue to breathe the breath of life on my marriage because it has been set apart and consecrated to the Lord to give Him glory. We don't want to build our house we want God to build it. God is the key to any successful marriage. If you don't have God in it, then don't you get in it? Know that there are going to be times that your husband is going to make you mad, and if you don't have God you may go out and do something stupid. You must remember marriage is a covenant of three; the Lord, you and him. You can't jump up and say I'm getting out of this relationship because it's not about you. When I got married I just didn't get married to have sex, I got married because two are better than one and a threefold cord is not easily broken. (Ecclesiastes 4:9) I look at marriage as a ministry. We have had our ups and down, but truly I know that this is the man God gave me. He loves God and he is a humble man. There is no other man amongst flesh that compares to my husband, but nobody can be compared to my God.

Chapter Eight

YOU ARE PRICELESS: SOLD OUT

Young lady you are priceless. There is no diamond ring, no hairdo, no designer-made purse or clothes that can value you. I don't know what it is about our generation but we have become like the latest fashion trend. You can have me if you pay my telephone bill, get my nails done, rent us an apartment, or let me drive your car. It's all about who has the latest shoes and who has the latest Dooney&Bourke, or my boyfriend got me this and my boyfriend bought me that. You need to understand, nothing is free. Your boyfriend is not doing these things for free, he wants something in return. You may be saying, no he does this because he loves me, but remember if he loved you, nine times out of ten when he's buying you all of this stuff, you are probably sexually involved with him. He may even be a little controlling. Watch out for these relationships. We are living in a dangerous time. These days some guys have the mindset of if I can't have you no one will. Surely you have heard about relationships ending up deadly when an individual tries to exit the relationship. Be careful, you are priceless.

I remember when I was dating my husband. He sent me $20 in the mail. I told him, "I don't take money from boys." He became offended and replied, "Boy? I am not a boy, I am a man." In my mind however, I felt like if you give me something you're going to want something back. He then explained to me that he was not like that. Well, I eventually spent the money on something for the church, but I wanted him to know that I don't care what you buy me I am still not giving you nothing. Young ladies, you are not for sale. You cannot be bought or purchased with any tangible gift.

See the devil is just like that; he will offer you things, but there is a catch. He tried Jesus like that. The Bible said that Jesus had fasted forty days and forty nights and afterward he was hungered. (Matthew 4:2) The devil tried to trick him three times. He told Jesus all the things he could offer Him if he would worship him, but Jesus had it all anyway, so He didn't need anything from the devil. Just like you have all you need in God, you don't need any of the temporary things the devil has to offer. Yes, the devil has things to offer you, but remember, he doesn't give you anything for free and sometimes the price you have to pay may cost you your life. The Bible says don't be ignorant concerning his devices. He is a trickster, and his mission is to deceive you. Do not allow yourself to fall into his trap because he will lead you to a place that you will not enjoy.

Chapter Nine

You've Got to Love Yourself

The Bible says in Jeremiah, Chapter 1, "Before you were formed in your mother's womb I knew you, and ordained you and set you apart." You were not a mistake. Maybe mom and dad got together not intending to produce a child. Maybe you were born out of bad circumstances, but whatever the case may be, you are here, and God has a purpose for you. We live in a mean society. It bases everything on looks. If you are not 5'11, 123 pounds and have beautiful skin, then you are not what the world considers pretty, but the devil is a liar, you are beautiful, and you better know it. A guy will treat you how you treat yourself. In a recent survey I asked a twenty-year-old guy, "From a guy's point of view, why do guys pressure girls?" He stated that, "Some guys are like children after cookies. They'll beg, plead, and cry until you give them what they want, but once you give it up they lose the respect." Young ladies, are you willing to give up your virginity at the cost of losing the respect of the person you gave it up to? I'd rather have respect any day. Choosing respect has nothing to do with looks. If you respect yourself you can get any guy you want, no matter what anyone else thinks, and he will honor you. I wrote a song a few years ago for also young ladies, and myself during a time when I really didn't love myself. I just didn't feel good about myself. I began to think about a comment that was made about me and it wasn't until I got older that it began to affect me. The song says I promise to love myself. Have you ever looked in the mirror and didn't like what you saw? Then you looked to your neighbor and said why it couldn't be me. Then you looked to your momma and asked, "Where's my daddy?" Then you looked to yourself again and wondered, "Why do I feel trapped?" If you're searching, trying to find your identity, just go to the word of God, then you will see that it is not about color, size or shape; all it's about is doing it God's way. See young ladies we all have issues. The Bible declares, "I will praise you for I was wonderfully and fearfully made, marvelous are your works and that my souls knows very well."(Psalm 139:14). He says my frame was not hidden for you, meaning God made you just like He wanted you to be. If He wanted you to be a certain color, He would have made you like that. There is nobody else like you. You don't have to be like anyone else. Just be you, fall in love with yourself, so that when God does send you your mate, he won't be in love with all the people you are trying to be. Instead, he will be in love with you, because you would have discovered your true identity. Everything you see on TV is not reality. A lot of images you see of women is just that; images, imaginations and technology. Don't get me wrong, there are some beautiful young ladies out there, but you are beautiful and there is not another like you. What I am trying to say is that just because a person looks like they have it together on the outside doesn't mean that there is no inner struggle. Any time God is not on the inside there is going to be a struggle. Haven't you seen beautiful actresses say how they have dealt with low self-esteem and how they wanted to end their life after a break-up? Look at how many divorces there are in Hollywood; they change spouses like they change their clothes. There is no reverence for marriage anymore. These are some of the same women that you admire, and aspire to look and be like, but they don't even want to be like themselves, because they don't have a personal relationship with themselves. You can tell me I am pretty all day long, but if I don't see myself like that, it is in vain. I have to see myself as being something first in order to celebrate me. It starts from the inside out. My heart grieves when I think about our youth today. I see so many young girls getting caught up. I know that you are faced with so many challenges. Some of them you were just born into. I know you may feel like you are trapped and there is no way out, but there is a better, actually, there is only one way. I found out that without God you cannot make it in this world. He is the source of your success. He fills the void that you have been trying to fill. Young ladies, I really don't know where I would be without the Lord. I really don't know how I could live in this world. I told you earlier that my grandmother is deceased; only by the grace of God am I still here. I know I could not write this book if I didn't know the Lord, but I am so glad that God allowed my grandparents to raise me. My mind goes back to the many times as a little girl how they showed me so much love. That's why I didn't have to go searching for love because I had it at home. I know a lot of you don't feel loved; you have to love yourself. I dare you to get to know the lover himself, Jesus Christ. He is the only one that can love you, teach you to love yourself and teach someone else how to love you.

Chapter Ten

It was Worth the Wait

I met my husband in August 1993 at my family's church in Fort Lauderdale, after attending my father's funeral. I was fifteen- years- old, and I had been saved for two years. He was up testifying about God's goodness, and I was shocked because I had never seen a young person, especially a young man, talking about the Lord. So, I innocently wrote him a letter just encouraging him to continue to serve God. I gave him my address and asked him to write me sometimes if he could, because I lived about 200 miles away from him at that time. Well, on September 4, 1993 (can you believe I still remember?) I received his letter in the mail. I was very excited. From then on, we wrote letter after letter. I believe that because I was saved my grandparents had trust in me, and I wanted to please them. I believe that's probably the only reason I was able to even communicate with him, plus the fact that he was so far away and I didn't go to Fort Lauderdale that often. I remember the first time he came to visit me. I had asked my grandparents if he could come for Christmas. I was so nervous that day. I had asked my uncle who was like a father figure to me if he could stay with him, because you know my granddaddy and grandma weren't going to let him stay at our house. We dated for six years, long distance. He took me out on my first date when I was twenty-years- old, in a limo. We went to Red Lobster about 20 miles from where I lived. I still wasn't sure about him because even after six years, I still needed to make sure he was the one. After the date I gave him a kiss on the cheek and said, "Thank you for the date." That was it. We sat outside on the porch until my uncle came and got him. I appreciated the date but I wasn't giving up anything.

Nineteen ninety-eight was a very hard year for me. My grandparents were telling me it was time for me to grow up and become a woman. I didn't understand at that time, but little did I know God was just preparing me for the deaths of my grandparents that would occur three years later. They were all I had ever known. My church and job were going through transitions and I didn't know what to do. I was seeking advice from everyone but it was still my decision. I had to make the choice. Grandma wanted me to move to Fort Lauderdale. I understand now what God was doing, but not then. That was a very difficult time in my life. I had received prophecy that if I moved away, I would never be anything, and that I shouldn't even marry my husband. I was so mentally messed up; I didn't want to mess up my life. Wauchula was so familiar to me. I knew everyone, and everybody knew me. If I moved I would be in an unfamiliar place and that was scary. Ultimately, God gave me one scripture and that was Proverbs 3:5, "Trust in the Lord with all your heart and lean not unto your own understanding. In all your ways acknowledge him and he will direct your paths." I stepped out on faith and moved and I was taught something; the same God that was in Wauchula, I brought Him with me and just because I left home I didn't leave Him.

On December 8, 1998 I moved to Fort Lauderdale, Florida with my mother. I was kind of concerned about the move because I had never stayed with my mother and I didn't know how the experience was going to be. I basically went to work and church, and spent time with Brian (fiancé). My mom and I have become closer and we have become like best friends. She is the funniest woman I know and I am blessed to have a mother like her. We are so much alike it's kind of scary. We even have the same voice. When someone calls her house and I answer the phone, they give me all the information because they think that I am her. I lived with her for eight months.

When living with my mother, it was different from when I was seeing my future husband twice a month, or three times a year. I saw him everyday all the time. I began to feel things I never felt before and to be honest I was afraid. There were times when I wanted to go back home because that was safety for me. I didn't want to be fornicating, because I had been preaching every since I was sixteen and I preached about fornication and waiting until God sends you your husband before having sex. I was determined to live what I preached and I wasn't going to allow anything to keep me from it. I desired to please God more than having sex. I encourage everyone; don't ever think that you are exempt from temptations. Also, don't play with the devil because he is not playing with you. He wants to take you out. He will use your weak flesh, and before you know it you would have done something so quick, you would have no idea how it happened. If it happened to King David who was a man after God's own heart, you better believe we have to be careful and not put ourselves in vulnerable situations. Go out in groups and return home in those groups. Don't try to be by yourself, it is not wise. For the Bible says, "Be sober and vigilant, because your adversary walks about as a roaring lion seeking whom he may devour." My husband never pressured me to do anything; it's your flesh alone that wants to sin. I can honestly say that God kept me. When I married my husband on August 21, 1999 I was a virgin, to God be the glory. We now have two children, Destiny seven-years-old and Brian, Jr. two-years-old and maybe a couple more in the near future. We also recently celebrated our 9th year wedding anniversary. That's the reason I want to encourage you. Young ladies, you don't have to do what everyone else is doing, you can choose to be different. It may not be popular but you will be respected. Even though you may feel like you gave up some good guys, you'll be glad at the end. Because, instead of them saying, "I hit that," they'll say,

"It's something different about her. She's not like the other girls." You are worth the wait.

Conclusion

As I close this book, I want to once again encourage you to fall in love with Jesus, make him your first priority. Give every hurt of your past to him. Every negative word that has ever been spoken over your life we reverse it and send it back to the pits of Hell. Wait on God; don't try to grow up too fast. The Bible says that there is a time and a season for all things. (Ecclesiastes 3:1) Take your time and enjoy your childhood. If you are not already 18 or older you'll be grown soon. Obey your parents. I know every home doesn't have the traditional family of a biological mother and biological father, but whatever your family structure is, be obedient and do what is right. Some of you may have to become the light in your family. If this is true, pray for your family and ask God to save them. Remember your parents have issues too and they may be dealing with some hurts of their past that may be affecting your relationship with them. Last but definitely not least, to sum up everything; young people, the greatest decision that you can ever make is to give God the best years of your life, give him your youth. The Bible declares in Ecclesiastes 12:1, "Remember your creator in the days of your youth, before the difficult days come, and the years draw nigh unto you."

"You're Worth The Wait" Questions

1. What does Romans 12:1 say?

2. What does Psalm 124:2 say?

*3. What do the words **worth** and **value** mean to you?*

4. *What does Jeremiah 29:11 say?*

____

____

____

____

____

5. *Why do worthy guys like a challenge?*

____

____

____

____

____

6. *What does 1st Timothy 4:12 say?*

____

____

____

____

____

7. What does Romans 3:4 say?

____

____

____

____

____

8. What do you like about yourself? What don't you like about yourself?

____

____

____

____

____

9. What makes you different from other girls?

____

____

____

____

____

10. Why should we meditate on God's word?

11. What does 1 Corinthians 10:13 say?

12. What does Corinthians 5:16 say?

13. What does the Bible mean when it says you were bought with a price? See 1 Corinthians 6:19

14. What does Psalm 32:10 say?

15. What does 1 John 4:8 say?

16. What does Corinthians 2:11 say?

17. Why is it important to know God first before you know the man?

18. What does 2 Timothy 2:22 say?

19. Why should you wait before you have sex?

____

____

____

____

____

20. What is the AIDS epidemic?

____

____

____

____

____

21. Has anyone close to you ever died of Aids? If so how did you deal with the situation?

____

____

____

____

____

22. What does the Bible say about love in 1 Corinthians, Chapter 13?

____

____

____

____

____

23. List some qualities that you want in a man?

____

____

____

____

____

Goals and Objectives

24. Where do you see yourself in 1 month?

____

____

____

____

____

25. Where do you see yourself in 3 months?

26. What does 2 Corinthians 5:17 say?

27. What does Romans 3:23 say?

28. What does Romans7: 15 say?

___

___

___

___

___

29. What does Matthew 12:43 say?

___

___

___

___

___

30. Read the book of Proverbs, Chapter 31 and meditate on it.

___

___

___

___

___

31. What does Psalm 127:1 say?

32. Why do you think there are so many divorces?

33. What does Ecclesiastes 4: 12 say?

34. What does 1 Peter 2:9 say?

35. Do you think it's OK to receive gifts from guys?

36. Has a guy every asked you to do something you know would hurt your parents if they found out?

37. What are some of the tricks of the devil?

38. What does John 14:6 say?

39. Read Jeremiah, Chapter 1

40. What does Psalm 139:14 say?

41. What is low self-esteem?

42. Do you think that your self-esteem is high or low? Explain

43. Have you had a personal experience with God? Explain

44. What does it mean to be searching for love in all the wrong places?

45. Do you feel loved? Why or Why Not

46. How has this society made you feel as it relates to outward beauty?

47. Do you believe in love at first sight?

48. How do you feel about premarital sex?

49. What does 1 Thessalonians 5:6 say?

50. Can you remain sexually pure without God? Explain your answer.

51. When guys mention your name, what do you want them to say about you?

52. What kind of guys are you attracted to?

53. Do you think that it's ok to be a virgin?

54. What are some pressures that you receive from peers?

55. How is your relationship with your mother?

____

____

____

____

____

56. How is your relationship with your father?

____

____

____

____

____

57. List three things that make you happy?

____

____

____

____

____

58. List three things that make you sad?

59. What is anger?

60. What does the acronym MADE (My Attitude Determines Everything) mean to you?

61. Can the choices you make today affect you tomorrow, and if so, What type of choices should you be making?

Common Sexually Transmitted Diseases

C	A	E	H	R	O	N	N	O	G
H	H	P	V	W	U	H	R	X	E
E	E	L	Q	E	I	I	F	F	N
P	R	N	A	D	L	V	S	N	I
A	P	M	I	M	J	A	Y	X	T
T	E	M	S	D	Y	I	P	M	A
I	S	J	H	L	N	D	H	L	L
T	F	F	F	S	D	S	I	F	W
I	V	I	C	N	K	Y	L	A	A
S	U	T	B	D	R	P	I	D	R
B	U	D	C	M	E	V	S	X	T

CHLAMYDIA HERPES GENITAL WART PID

HEPATITIS B HIV/ AIDS SYPHILIS GONNORHEA

1. What is Chlamydia?

2. What are Genital Warts?

3. What is Hepatitis B?

4. What Is (PID) Pelvic Inflammatory Disease?

5. What is Syphilis?

6. What is HIV/AIDS?

7. What is Gonorrhea?

1. God is against pre-marital sex.	*T or F*
2. Sex is a bad thing.	*T or F*
3. Lust and Love is the same thing.	*T or F*
4. My boyfriend won't leave me if I get pregnant.	*T or F*
5. I can get HIV the first time I have sex.	*T or F*
6. God will not forgive me if I have premarital sex.	*T or F*
7. Sex can only affect me physically not emotionally.	*T or F*
8. God created sex between male and female.	*T or F*
9. God will never leave you nor forsake you.	*T or F*
10. God hates the sin but he loves you.	*T or F*
11. God doesn't want you to ever have sex.	*T or F*
12. HIV/Aids does not kill teenagers	*T or F*
13. Boys respect girls who give it up easy.	*T or F*
14. God created me for a purpose.	*T or F*
15. I am not a virgin, but I can still wait.	*T or F*
16. Skinny girls are prettier than bigger girls.	*T or F*
17. My body is the temple of the Holy Ghost	*T or F*
18. I was fearfully and wonderfully made.	*T or F*
19. Real love will wait.	*T or F*
20. Marriage is honorable in the eyesight of God.	*T or F*

"YOU'RE WORTH THE WAIT"

TOOLS TO USE

10 lies of the devil

10 ways to respond

1. *If you love me you will do it.*

    If you love me you would wait.

2. *We're getting married soon.*

    But we are not married yet.

3. *Nobody doesn't want you but me.*

    God wants me and I want myself.

4. *I am not ready to get saved.*

    You're not ready to be with me.

5. *I don't want to wait.*

    Well, you are not my mate.

6. *Let's do it this one time and not any more.*

    That may be one time too many.

7. *I know plenty of girls that will give it up.*

    Good, go and get one.

8. *We already did it so what's the difference.*

    I am different.

9. *I'll get saved for you.*

    No, you need to get saved for yourself.

10. *Everybody makes mistakes.*

    And I am learning from mine.

Don't Hate Celebrate
Building Self Esteem

What is self Esteem?

Name 5 things you like about yourself, include your features such as ,eyes, hair, skin, etc.

1.______________________________

2.______________________________

3.______________________________

4.______________________________

5.______________________________

What does society consider pretty and what does society consider ugly? Do you agree with society?

Do you compare yourself to other girls based upon society view of them?

Yes or No

Why or Why Not

What is inner Beauty?

Testimonies of Some Who Are Waiting

I grew up in a loving Christian home, and sex was always discussed and thought of as something you did when you were married. When I was in third grade however, my parents got divorced and it caused a lot of pain in my life for the following six years. I got to the point that the ONLY thing I could rely on was God. He was my Abba Father. Without Him, I don't know if I would have made it through. I say this because I know many of my own friends that are searching to be loved by a man (many times because they didn't have their own father in the home growing up). God can restore and heal like no one else. He is always calling us to Him and can fill huge voids that have been left empty.

It wasn't until I was in middle school that living a lifestyle of purity (not just not having sex) started to make sense and became something I wanted to do. I stopped dressing immodest like so many of my other girlfriends and I committed to God to not have sex until I was married (which was the first step). I understood God has a plan for my life and if a husband were part of that plan then it would be better than anything I could dream up myself!

In high school I was one of those girls that had a lot of guy friends but never really dated. Now as a college student, I am so glad that I didn't date around. I got to hang out with guys and have quality friendships without the fear that they were spending time with me to see what they could physically get. I believe I saved my heart from a lot of the emotional baggage that comes with dating and breaking-up, dating and breaking-up. My favorite verse about God's plan of forgiveness for when we mess up (and no one is perfect) is 1 John 1: 9, "If we confess our sins, he is faithful and just and will forgive us our sins and purify us from all unrighteousness."

Now I am twenty-two and a senior in college. I am dating someone and we are committed to not only saving sex until we get married, but also to live out the life we know God is calling both of us to in our dating relationship—a lifestyle (body and mind) of purity. Because we are both equally committed to saving sex for marriage, and not getting into make-out sessions, we recognize that even our kisses are valuable. It has taken a lot of the pressure away from waiting. It's not always easy, but I know it will ALL be worth it!

— Kristin, 22

Although it had always been an unspoken expectation in my family to remain abstinent 'til marriage, I don't think I really made it my own until I was a freshman in high school. I just knew that there were things that God had for me as I pursued sexual purity that couldn't happen otherwise. Another turning point was my freshman year at UF where I decided that I did not want to kiss any other girl but the one who I married. There were times when I was an undergrad at the University of Florida and while I was in the Navy that some girls put me in a situation that a young man might dream about apart from God. Somehow when I needed the strength the Holy Spirit gave me strength. Looking back, I don't know how I made it through when I look back at some of those situations except by strength from the Holy Spirit. In retrospect, I think the commitment to abstinence has been easier than the ever-present battle to keep my eyes from sinning against God. I want to encourage every young person not just to abstain physically but also to pay attention to what goes in through your eyes and ears. Are we saying one thing yet doing another? We need to continually ask ourselves that. I am now 26 years old and still a virgin. I know that there is a woman for me that God has that has made a similar commitment to purity.

— Vineet, 26 Grad Student

My name is Brother Stephan Davis and I have decided to wait because I understand that God has endowed me with a GIFT, WHICH is being a virgin. I also know that this special ness is only for a SPECIAL (my wife) person.

— Stephan, 16

My name is Brittany Goodwin and I have DECIDED to wait. I am making this decision because of the AIDS rate. I also think that by me waiting, it would be a great gift to my husband other than my love for him. Additionally I consider myself to be a role model for younger girls and I wouldn't want to lead them down the wrong path by introducing them to sexual activities.

— Brittany, 17

The Bible says that a man that findeth a wife findeth a good thing, and I do consider myself to be a good thing. Unfortunately I lost my virginity at an early age and became another statistic. If it had not been for the lord who looked beyond my faults and conformed me in spite of what I did, I don't know where I would be. Due to that awesome restoration that God made in my life; who wouldn't serve a God like that? I now consider myself to have a personal relationship with God and I try not to compromise my salvation for two minutes of pleasure and confusion. I say confusion because being a child of God, conviction is the best thing that happened to me and I became confused because I knew that in the world's eyes, sex is something that is pleasure to the married and unmarried. But I knew better and that is where conviction took place. You know how they say if you lay with a dog you get fleas, well that's what happened to me. Not only was I carrying my Spirit, but also I had taken on other spirits, which made it harder for me to grow in God. But to God be the glory I don't have fleas any more. I refuse to go about my life being a victim of

Heartbreak, Pain, Depression, and Disease and also unwanted Past Memories. I know that if I wait on God I can have all the things that he desires for me to have because I know that it is not my will but his will that needs to be done in my life. I have decided to wait because I know if I stay connected with God he will connect me with the man that he has for me. This is why I made up my mind to **Wait!!!!**

— Charde, 17

Hey Kim, I read your book and it was beyond my expectations. I can honestly say that it enlightened me in a lot of ways. I liked how you used past experiences to try and relate to my time of day. You showed emotion. Your attitude was somewhat a serene but serious urge that had let me know that you were concerned and cared. You gripped my attention by being concerned so I kept on reading. You addressed a lot of issues us teens face during our lifetime. In Chapter Two, you started by defining the word "Worth". We often don't know what our worth is. For me, you helped me realize what I never did about myself. During this time teenagers start relationships without any reason on why they want to be involved in this kind of bond. Their real reason (and once mine) is sex. They don't know what it takes to actually build a relationship. You identified the characteristics of a real relationship and succeeded to inform me to love Jesus first. Then when I have done that, he will reveal to me who I am and with that opening view I can proceed into further significant involvements. You also stressed the importance of "Waiting." When I read what you said it made sense. It made me remember that good things come to those that wait and nothing worth having is easy One more thing that I want you to know. I didn't wait. I felt kind of bad because I thought it was too late to wait. I understand now that it's not. In your book, I noticed that you did not judge. You let me know that I have a second chance to do right. Your book was inspirational to me.

I decided to wait because it is less risk of catching a disease or becoming pregnant. There are more things in life to focus on than sex.

(Lakesha Thompson, 17)

I decided to wait because I felt like nobody deserved my body. Anybody who can't wait on me isn't worth me. I also want to know that whomever I give my body to was worth it. I want to know that I won't end up regretting my decision.

(Pamela McElvy, 17)

I feel as if my body is my precious temple. Anyone who is to take my pureness away from me should wait until I'm ready.

(LaTonya Joseph, 17)

I wanted to wait because my dreams are too big for me to mess them up over intercourse.

(Ashley King, 17)

"You're Worth The Wait"

Journal

Name

You're Worth the Wait

<u>Journal</u>

Who can find a virtuous woman for her worth is far above rubies? Proverbs 31:10

You're Worth the Wait

Journal

Who can find a virtuous woman for her worth is far above rubies? Proverbs 31:10

You're Worth the Wait

Journal

Who can find a virtuous woman for her worth is far above rubies? Proverbs 31:10

You're Worth the Wait

Journal

Who can find a virtuous woman for her worth is far above rubies? Proverbs 31:10

You're Worth the Wait

<u>Journal</u>

Who can find a virtuous woman for her worth is far above rubies? Proverbs 31:10

You're Worth the Wait

Journal

Who can find a virtuous woman for her worth is far above rubies? Proverbs 31:10

You're Worth the Wait

Journal

Who can find a virtuous woman for her worth is far above rubies? Proverbs 31:10

You're Worth the Wait

Journal

Who can find a virtuous woman for her worth is far above rubies? Proverbs 31:10

You're Worth the Wait

Journal

Who can find a virtuous woman for her worth is far above rubies? Proverbs 31:10

You're Worth the Wait

<u>Journal</u>

Who can find a virtuous woman for her worth is far above rubies? Proverbs 31:10

You're Worth the Wait

<u>Journal</u>

Who can find a virtuous woman for her worth is far above rubies? Proverbs 31:10

You're Worth the Wait

Journal

Who can find a virtuous woman for her worth is far above rubies? Proverbs 31:10

You're Worth the Wait

Journal

Who can find a virtuous woman for her worth is far above rubies? Proverbs 31:10

You're Worth the Wait

Journal

____

Who can find a virtuous woman for her worth is far above rubies? Proverbs 31:10

You're Worth the Wait

<u>Journal</u>

Who can find a virtuous woman for her worth is far above rubies? Proverbs 31:10

You're Worth the Wait

Journal

Who can find a virtuous woman for her worth is far above rubies? Proverbs 31:10

You're Worth the Wait

Journal

Who can find a virtuous woman for her worth is far above rubies? Proverbs 31:10

You're Worth the Wait

Journal

Who can find a virtuous woman for her worth is far above rubies? Proverbs 31:10

You're Worth the Wait

Journal

Who can find a virtuous woman for her worth is far above rubies? Proverbs 31:10

You're Worth the Wait

Journal

Who can find a virtuous woman for her worth is far above rubies? Proverbs 31:10

You're Worth the Wait

Journal

Who can find a virtuous woman for her worth is far above rubies? Proverbs 31:10

You're Worth the Wait

Journal

Who can find a virtuous woman for her worth is far above rubies? Proverbs 31:10

You're Worth the Wait

Journal

Who can find a virtuous woman for her worth is far above rubies? Proverbs 31:10

You're Worth the Wait

Journal

Who can find a virtuous woman for her worth is far above rubies? Proverbs 31:10

You're Worth the Wait

Journal

Who can find a virtuous woman for her worth is far above rubies? Proverbs 31:10

You're Worth the Wait

Journal

Who can find a virtuous woman for her worth is far above rubies? Proverbs 31:10

You're Worth the Wait

<u>Journal</u>

Who can find a virtuous woman for her worth is far above rubies? Proverbs 31:10

You're Worth the Wait

Journal

Who can find a virtuous woman for her worth is far above rubies? Proverbs 31:10

You're Worth the Wait

Journal

Who can find a virtuous woman for her worth is far above rubies? Proverbs 31:10

You're Worth the Wait

Journal

Who can find a virtuous woman for her worth is far above rubies? Proverbs 31:10

You're Worth the Wait

<u>Journal</u>

Who can find a virtuous woman for her worth is far above rubies? Proverbs 31:10

You're Worth the Wait

Journal

Who can find a virtuous woman for her worth is far above rubies? Proverbs 31:10

You're Worth the Wait

Journal

Who can find a virtuous woman for her worth is far above rubies? Proverbs 31:10

You're Worth the Wait

Journal

Who can find a virtuous woman for her worth is far above rubies? Proverbs 31:10

You're Worth the Wait

<u>Journal</u>

Who can find a virtuous woman for her worth is far above rubies? Proverbs 31:10

You're Worth the Wait

Journal

Who can find a virtuous woman for her worth is far above rubies? Proverbs 31:10

You're Worth the Wait

<u>Journal</u>

Who can find a virtuous woman for her worth is far above rubies? Proverbs 31:10

You're Worth the Wait

Journal

Who can find a virtuous woman for her worth is far above rubies? Proverbs 31:10

You're Worth the Wait

Journal

Who can find a virtuous woman for her worth is far above rubies? Proverbs 31:10

You're Worth the Wait

Journal

Who can find a virtuous woman for her worth is far above rubies? Proverbs 31:10

You're Worth the Wait

Journal

Who can find a virtuous woman for her worth is far above rubies? Proverbs 31:10

You're Worth the Wait

Journal

Who can find a virtuous woman for her worth is far above rubies? Proverbs 31:10

You're Worth the Wait

<u>Journal</u>

Who can find a virtuous woman for her worth is far above rubies? Proverbs 31:10

You're Worth the Wait

Journal

Who can find a virtuous woman for her worth is far above rubies? Proverbs 31:10

You're Worth the Wait

Journal

Who can find a virtuous woman for her worth is far above rubies? Proverbs 31:10

You're Worth the Wait

Journal

Who can find a virtuous woman for her worth is far above rubies? Proverbs 31:10

You're Worth the Wait

<u>Journal</u>

Who can find a virtuous woman for her worth is far above rubies? Proverbs 31:10

You're Worth the Wait

Journal

Who can find a virtuous woman for her worth is far above rubies? Proverbs 31:10

You're Worth the Wait

<u>Journal</u>

Who can find a virtuous woman for her worth is far above rubies? Proverbs 31:10

You're Worth the Wait

Journal

Who can find a virtuous woman for her worth is far above rubies? Proverbs 31:10

You're Worth the Wait

<u>Journal</u>

Who can find a virtuous woman for her worth is far above rubies? Proverbs 31:10

You're Worth the Wait

Journal

Who can find a virtuous woman for her worth is far above rubies? Proverbs 31:10

You're Worth the Wait

<u>Journal</u>

Who can find a virtuous woman for her worth is far above rubies? Proverbs 31:10

You're Worth the Wait

Journal

Who can find a virtuous woman for her worth is far above rubies? Proverbs 31:10

You're Worth the Wait

<u>Journal</u>

Who can find a virtuous woman for her worth is far above rubies? Proverbs 31:10

You're Worth the Wait

Journal

Who can find a virtuous woman for her worth is far above rubies? Proverbs 31:10

You're Worth the Wait

<u>Journal</u>

Who can find a virtuous woman for her worth is far above rubies? Proverbs 31:10

You're Worth the Wait

Journal

Who can find a virtuous woman for her worth is far above rubies? Proverbs 31:10

You're Worth the Wait

<u>Journal</u>

Who can find a virtuous woman for her worth is far above rubies? Proverbs 31:10

You're Worth the Wait

Journal

Who can find a virtuous woman for her worth is far above rubies? Proverbs 31:10

You're Worth the Wait

Journal

Who can find a virtuous woman for her worth is far above rubies? Proverbs 31:10

You're Worth the Wait

Journal

Who can find a virtuous woman for her worth is far above rubies? Proverbs 31:10

You're Worth the Wait

<u>Journal</u>

Who can find a virtuous woman for her worth is far above rubies? Proverbs 31:10

You're Worth the Wait

Journal

Who can find a virtuous woman for her worth is far above rubies? Proverbs 31:10

You're Worth the Wait

Journal

Who can find a virtuous woman for her worth is far above rubies? Proverbs 31:10

You're Worth the Wait

Journal

Who can find a virtuous woman for her worth is far above rubies? Proverbs 31:10

You're Worth the Wait

<u>Journal</u>

Who can find a virtuous woman for her worth is far above rubies? Proverbs 31:10

You're Worth the Wait

Journal

Who can find a virtuous woman for her worth is far above rubies? Proverbs 31:10

You're Worth the Wait

<u>Journal</u>

Who can find a virtuous woman for her worth is far above rubies? Proverbs 31:10

Additional Resources

Teen Hotlines:

CDC National Aids/STDs Hotline: 1800-342-2437

National Teen Emergency Hotline: 1-800-448-3000

Covenant House Nineline: 1-800-999-9999

National Domestic Violence Hotline: 1-800-821-4357

National Sexual Assault Hotline: 1-800-656-4673

USA National Suicide Hotline: 1-800-784-2433

National Suicide Talk Hotline: 1-800-273-8255

National Human Trafficking Hotline: 1-888-373-7888

Safe Place: 1-888-290-7233

Teen websites:

www.teenhelp.com

www.advocatesforyouth.org

www.kidshealth.org

www.truth4teens.org

Educational websites:

www.fafsa.ed.gov

www.scholarships.com

www.fastweb.com

www.blackexcel.org/100minority.htm

Success

Success is not measured by how many degrees you can obtain nor is it measured by who knows your name. Success is not measured by how much money you can make or how many people you can tear down for your namesake. But success is measured by knowing who God is and who He is in you and acknowledging Him in everything you do. So walk by Faith and not by sight because true success only comes when you meditate on God's word both Day and Night.

"You're Worth The Wait" Vow

From this day forward I, ______________________________ vow to wait for my wedding date before having sex. I commit myself to live a life of purification and holiness to the Lord, and will honor Him with my body, soul, and mind. Amen.

Made in the USA
Columbia, SC
27 May 2019